SQL For Beginners

Comprehensive Programming Guide for Learning SQL Languages, Coding, Data Science and Mastering Databases (2022 Crash Course For All)

Shane Black

Table of Contents

Chapters 1. What is SQL Programming and Coding? 11

Chapters 2. Language of data Definition 31

Chapters 3. What is data Description Language? 52

Chapters 4. Learn more about adding, Removing, and Updating Data. 58

Chapters 5. How to secure data from SQL Tables 68

Chapters 6. SQL joins and union 91

Chapters 7. Transactions in SQL Server 105

Because of the more complex information that these businesses must store, a new 'Relational Database Management System' has been created to assist in keeping this information safe in a way that the DBMS has not been able to.

Now, as a business owner, you have some diferent alternatives to choose from if you want to get a good database management system. Most business owners use SQL since it is one of the best solutions available. The SQL language is simple to use, was designed to work well with businesses, and will provide you with all of the tools you need to ensure the security of your data. Let's spend some more time looking at this SQL and learning how to make it work for your business.

It is best to begin at the beginning. SQL is a computer language that stands for 'Structured Query Language,' and it is a simple language to learn because it allows interaction across different databases in the same system. This database system first appeared in the 1970s, but it wasn't until IBM released its own prototype of this programming language that it really began to gain popularity and the business world began to take notice.

The initial version of SQL used by IBM, known back then as ORACL, was so successful that the team behind it eventually left IBM and became its own firm. ORACL, because of its ability to deal with SQL, is still one of the leaders in programming languages, and it is always changing to keep up with everything that is needed in the programming and database management field. SQL is a set of instructions that you can use to communicate with your relational database. While there are several languages you may use to do this, SQL is the only language that most databases understand. When you're ready to interact with one of these databases, the software can go in and translate the commands you give it, whether they're in form entries or mouse clicks. These will be translated into SQL statements, which the database will already be able to interpret.

If you've ever worked with a database-driven software program, you've probably used some kind of SQL in the past. However, it is likely that you were unaware that you were doing so. There are several dynamic web pages that are database driven, for example. These will take some user input from the forms and clicks that you are doing and use it to create a SQL query. This query will then go through and retrieve information from the database in order to perform the action, such as switching to a new page.

Consider a simple online catalogue that allows you to search to demonstrate how this works. The search page will frequently have a form with only a text box. You can enter the name of the item that you want to search using the form, and then just click on the search button. When you click the search button, the web server will search through the database to locate anything related to that search term. It will return them to create a new web page that corresponds to your specific request.

For those who haven't spent much time learning a programming language and don't consider themselves programmers, the SQL commands aren't too difficult to learn. SQL commands are all written in a syntax that is compatible with the English language.

At first, this will appear to be very complicated, and you may be concerned about how much work it will take to get it set up. However, after you begin working on a few codes, you will see that it is not all that difficult to deal with. Often, simply reading the SQL statement will help you figure out what the command will accomplish. Take a look at the following code:

How does this interact with your database?

If you decide that SQL is the language you will use to manage your database, you can look at the database. When you look at this, you will notice that you are essentially just looking at groups of information. Some people will consider these to be organisational mechanisms that will be used to store information that you, the user, can look at later on, and it will do so as efficiently as possible. When it comes to managing your database, SQL may help you with a lot of things, and you will see some great results.

There are times when you are working on a project with your organisation and you may be working with a database that is quite similar to SQL and you may not even realise it. For example, a phone book is a type of database that is regularly used. This will have a wealth of information about people in your area, such as their NAMEe, the type of business they run, their address, and phone numbers. And because all of this information is in one place, you won't have to search all over to discover it.

This is similar to how the SQL database works. It will accomplish this by searching through the information stored in your company's database. It will sort through that information so that you can find what you need faster and without making a mess or losing time.

Client technology and server technology

Now, these systems were able to work, and they got the job done for a long time. If your organisation uses these and this is what you are most comfortable with, it gets the job done. However, there are other alternatives on the market that will perform a better job. These settings are available in the client-server system.

These systems will utlize diferent processes to help you get the results needed. With this one, the main computer that you are using, known as the'server,' will be accessible to any user on the network. Now, these users have to have the request credentials to do this, which helps keep the system safe and secure. However, if the user has the correct information and is connected to your network, they can reach the information with little trouble and effort. The user can get the server from other servers or from their desktop computer, and the user will then be recognised as the 'client' so that the client and server are easily

How to work with on-line databases

Many business owners will discover that client and server technology is the one that works best for them. This system is great for many companies, but there are some things that you may need to add or remove at times due to how technology has changed recently. Some companies like the idea that their database will perform better with the internet so that they can work on it no matter where they are, whether at home or at the office. There will be times when a customer will have an account with the company and will need to be able to access the database online as well. For example, if you have an

Amazon account, you are a member of their database and can acquire access to certain portions through this.

As the trend of companies migrating online continues, it is more typical to see databases moving online as well, and that you must have a website and a solid web browser so that customers can come in and check them out. You can always add user NAMEes and passwords to make it more secure and ensure that only the correct user has access to their information. This is a great way to protect your customers' personal and payment information. Most companies will requre their users to select security credentials to get on the account, but they will offer the account for free.

Of course, this is a simple system to work with, but there will be a number of things going on behind the scenes to ensure that the programme works properly. The customer can simply go onto the system and check the information, but the server will have a lot of work to do to ensure that the information is showing up on the screen correctly, and to ensure that the user has a nice experience and can see their own account information on the screen.

For example, you may be able to see that the web browser you are using uses SQL or a programme similar to it to figure out who the user is that your data is hoping to see. The SQL system will be used to access your database as soon as the customer enters what they are looking for.

Why is SQL so fantastic?

After discussing the many types of database management systems that you can work with, it is time to explore why you would prefer SQL over some of the other options available. You may deal with other databases as well as different coding languages, and there are advantages to using each one. So, why would you want to deal specifically with SQL? Some of the many benefits of adopting SQL as your database management system include:

Extremely quick

If you want to choose a management system that can quickly sort through information and return results, SQL is one of the best tools to use. You'll be surprised at how much information you can obtain and how soon it will be returned to you. In fact, of all the solutions available, this is the most efficient one.

Standards well defined

The database that comes with SQL ha been working well for a long time. Furthermore, it has been able to develop some good standards that ensure the database is strong and functions the way you want it to. Some of the other databases you might want to interact with will not support these standards, which might be frustrating when you use them.

You do not require a lot of coding.

If you're looking at SQL databases, you don't need to be a coding expert to get the job done. We shall look at a few codes that can help, but even a beginner will get them down and do well when working with SQL.

Keeps your belongings organised

When it comes to running your business, it is critical that you can keep your information safe, secure, and organised. And, while there are several great databases to choose from, none will function as well as the SQL language at getting this all done.

DBMS based on Objects

The SQL database relies on the DBMS system that we discussed earlier since it will make it easier to find the information that you are searching for, store the proper items, and perform so much more within the database.

The advantages that you can obtain if you choose to operate with the SQL programme. While some people struggle with this interface at first, there are a tonne of wonderful features to work on with SQL, and you will really enjoy how fast and easy it is to work with this language and its database.

CHAPTER 1. WHAT IS SQL PROGRAMMING AND CODING?

This chapter will provide you an overview of SQL's history, including why and how it came to be. Understanding the history of this computer language will help you understand its importance to most IT professionals who have decided to focus on acquiring expertise in the field of data management. Such knowledge will also guide you in maximising the potentials of the SQL language as a programming tool.

Investing in technology that will efficiently and effectively gather, analyze, manipulate, and present raw data into meaningful information is the major priority of practically all businesses nowadays - from small to large scale enterprises. A powerful data management technology will unquestionably provide a company with the expertise it requires to remain competitive, if not ahead of its competitors. That is why Structured Query Language, or SQL (pronounced "ess-que-el" or "see'qwl"), has been developed as a standard tool for database administrators, developers, or analysts to communicate with databases.

History of SQL

In the 1970s, an American multinational technology and consulting firm called International Business Machines Corporation, or simply IBM, invented a computer database language. The program's primary job was to collect, organise, and process databases. nhancement features, such as implementang and monitoring database security, were included in the computer software to improve its performance. When IBM researchers discovered that another firm was using the same "Sequel" trademark, it was reNAMEed SQL, which stands for Structured Query Language.

SQL had already gone through several versions since it was first released to the public. Each database software type or version can be identified by the developer who created the programme. Oracle Corporation, formerly known as Relational Software, Incorporated, released the first SQL product called ORACL in 1979. SQL has become an industry standard in the field of information technology due to the increasing demand for data management solutions (IT). This formal norm was further upheld by the International

Standards Organization, abbreviated ISO. SQL, as implemented by IBM, became the database communication benchmark in 1986. Another organisation, American National Standards Institute (ANSI), which authorizes certain standards in numerous US industries, developed another database application known as ANSI SQL. This was eventually adopted as one of the international standards by ISO in 1987. Further revisions of the standards, such as SQL-92 and SQL-99, were released in 1992 and 1999, respectively. The most recent one is currently known as SQL-2011, and it was formally released in December 2011. Finally, ANSI and ISO are the two international organisations that protect and maintain numerous SQL standards.

SQL Features

SQL, as previously said, is an ISO and ANSI standard database computer language that enables users to create, update, delete, retrieve, and present data in a meaningful manner. One may easily understand and learn the commands used in this programme, which were patterned in English. SQL statements that are commonly used are select, add, update, insert, delete, create, and alter. Because of the program's simplicity, handling databases is less complicated, as there is no need to write complex code. Furthermore, SQL is a comprehensive utility that can be used to efficiently and quickly retrieve large amounts of data from a database for analysis.

The following are some of the reasons why SQL has become the standard computer database management tool in practically every type of platform:

SQL may run in mainframes, personal computers (PCs), laptops, and even hand-held devices such as mobile phones, with or without internet connectivity. This also means that you can transfer databases from one device to another without encountering any issues.

Simple statements/commands - SQL structure is characterized as a declarative language, which mostly comprises of nglish statements, so that a novice user can easily begin programming in no time.

Interactive programming environment - SQL may be used right away to interact with databases and swiftly process complex commands.

Several data views - SQL gives different users multiple views of database content and structure.

DyNAMEic database access and definition with internet connectivity - **SQL** enables dyNAMEic changes to the database structure inside a three-tiered Internet architecture (client, application server, and a database), even if such database is being acce

SQL is a **complete database language** that provides all of the commands and functions needed to manipulate databases.

SQL has been designed to integrate with Java via an application programming interface (API) known as **Java Database Connectivity (JDBC).**

<u>**SQL-based Applications**</u>

Generally, when you download database application programmes, you must pay for them. However, there are several open-source SQL versions that are free to use and allow anyone to modify the original programme. However, these numerous versions are not exactly the same, and a database software or server is required to access and manipulate the data. As a result, most software vendors have created their own servers for such database applications.

With the current shift away from solely creating things and delivering services, the corporate sector is discovering novel methods to invest in powerful SQL database systems capable of managing massive volumes of data. The primary goal is to convert raw data into meaningful pieces of information that will lead to improved company processes. Such enhancements in data manipulation will generate more profitable business insights. One can also believe that only computer professionals, such as database administrators and developers, will benefit from using this all-powerful tool. It's worth noting that knowing even a little bit about SQL can help people in a variety of roles, from simple data encoders to database scientists. SQL is not only useful for programmers since its semantics enable non-IT personnel to understand the data flow and manipulation that drives every firm. Furthermore, stepping up your computer programming skills with this language opens several career opportunities, whether in the management, analytic, research, or IT fields.

ENVIRONMNT FUNDAMNTALS IN SQL

Structure of a Database

Before you can learn the technical aspects of SQL as a programming language, you must first understand what a database is and what its components are. A database can be defined and described in a variety of ways, but it is essentially a collection of items that have existed for a certain period of time. Consider a calling card holder to be a database that organises all of your business cards, each of which contains different information about different people (example: complete NAMEe, job title, company NAMEe, and contact details), whom you may or may not know personally. A database, according to a more professional definition, is an organised instrument capable of keeping data or information related to one another, which may be efficiently and effectively retrieved when the need arises.

A record is created when such conceptual information is represented digitally or physically. As an example, if you want to keep track of your business contacts, each business card will be assigned to a specific record that contains several pieces of information for a certain contact person. These pieces of information are now referred to as the record's attributes. Another element is metadata, which contains information that defines or describes the structure of the data in the database. To improve data retrieval and organisation, all of this information will be stored in a single region known as the data dictionary.

The illustration above illustrates how the database elements are integrated to one another. The database holds the information required by an organization's numerous users. Different objects, such as tables and views that present information in a more readable fashion, are created from these sets of data. Then there are the queries or inquiries into the database that will extract data and present it in accordance with the user's requirements. Finally, we have database processes that will handle other user requests.

Databases are also classified into three types based on their size, the machinery in which they run, and the size of the organisation that manages them:

- **Personal Database** – Cconceptualized and designed by a single person, this database is implemented on stand-alone computers. It has a simple structure and is relatively tiny in size. Your electronic personal address book is a example.

- **Workgroup/Deptmental Database** – This database, which was created by members of a certain workgroup or department within an organisation, is larger and more complex than the personal type. This can be accessed by multiple users at the same time.

- **Enterprise Database** - This type of database is capable of handling the entire flow of a massive information system required by very large enterprises. As a result, its design entails significantly more complex structures.

SQL Program Add-Ons

Before you begin coding in SQL, you must first understand its programming components. These components include the fundamental commands used in performing various database functions.

Language for Data Manipulation (DML)

This component is made up of SQL commands that handle data processing and maintenance tasks. This means that the user can select, enter, change, or remove data from the table. These are the four primary DML commands:

- **SELCT** – This command selects rows of data from a certain table.

- **INESRT** — This command inserts new data values or data rows into a certain table.

- **UPDATE** — This command modifies or alters pre-existing data values or data rows in a table. Within a database, a single table or several rows/columns of a certain table are updated.

- **DELETE** – This command is used to remove certain records or rows of data from the table (or even the entire table).

Language for Data Control (DCL)

This SQL component is made up of commands that allow the user to manage data access within the database using user privileges. Accidental or intentional misuse of information by database users is also avoided. All SQL statements that perform any database operation are captured and saved in a log file. The following are the primary DCL commands:

•	**GRANT** - This command grants a user specific privileges by granting him access to the database.

•	**REVOK** – This command removes a user's privileges or permission to access the database.

Now that you've become acquainted with the most popular SQL commands, the next step is to learn how to successfully install the software language into your PC or laptop. Before deciding which SQL version is appropriate for your device, you must first determine why you need a database. Too many design details will result in a very complex database, which will waste time and effort, as well as the storage space of your device. Inadequate detail specifications, on the other hand, will lead to a poor performance and inefficient database. Once you've completed the database design phase, you may decide which programming software to download to begin your SQL experience journey.

SQLite Configuration

You must have firsthand knowledge of SQLite in order to participate in this eBook's conversation. This is a simple software library that is recommended as a database engine starter for someone who is just starting out with designing, building, and deploying apps. SQLite, created by Richard Hipp and his team of programmers, is a free and stand-alone database software that is quick to download and simple to administrate.

These are some of the unique features of the SQLite database programming language:

- Server-less zero configuration - SQLite does not necessitate any special setup procedure while configuring files, nor does it necessitate a separate server process.

- Simple compilation with a readable source code - SQLite source code was designed to be simple and accessible, even for a average user.

• SQLite library is compact - it is no larger than 500KiB in size and has a very minimal code footprint. In addition, any unnecessary features are disabled at compile-time to further reduce the library's size.

• Stable Cross-Platform Database Portability - SQLite file format written on one development can be ued on another machine with a different architecture or platform. It was also designed to be stable and compatible at all times, so that newer versions of SQLite may read and write older database files.

If you want to learn a new coding language, you have a lot of different options to choose from, and it really depends on what you are searching for and what you want to accomplish with them. Some of these languages are useful for helping you create a good website. Some are better for beginners, while others are better for those who are more advanced. Some are useful for developing a smartphone app or creating your own game to share with others.

Traditionally, many businesses would use the 'Database Management System,' or DBMS, to help them stay organised and keep track of their customers and products. This was the first option on the market for this type of organisation, and it works well. However, over the years, there have been some newer methods that have changed the way that companies can sort and have their information. Even when it comes to the most basic data management system that you can use, you will notice that there is a lot more power and security than you would have found in the past.

Big companies will be responsible for retaining a large amount of data, some of which will include personal information about their customers such as address, NAMEe, and credit card information. Because of the more complex information that these businesses must store, a new 'Relational Database Management System' has been created to assist in keeping this information safe in a way that the DBMS has not been able to.

Now, as a buness owner, you have some diferent alternatives to choose from if you want to get a good database management system. Most business owners use SQL since it is one of the best solutions available. The SQL language is simple to use, was designed to work well with businesses, and will provide you with all of the tools you need to ensure the security of your data. Let's spend some more time looking at this SQL and learning how to make it work for your business.

WHAT EXACTLY IS SQL?

The initial version of SQL used by IBM, known back then as ORACL, was so successful that the team behind it eventually left IBM and became its own firm. ORACL, because of its ability to deal with SQL, is still one of the leaders in programming languages, and it is always changing to keep up with everything that is needed in the programming and database management field. SQL is a set of instructions that you can use to communicate with your relational database. While there are several languages you may use to do this, SQL is the only language that most databases understand. When you're ready to interact with one of these databases, the software can go in and translate the commands you give it, whether they're in form entries or mouse clicks. These will be translated into SQL statements, which the database will already be able to interpret.

There are three basic components, which will be discussed in further detail in the following chapter. However, the three primary ones will be 'Data Control Language,' 'Data Definition Language,' and 'Data Manipulation Language.'

If you've ever worked with a database-driven software programme, you've probably used some kind of SQL in the past. However, it is likely that you were unaware that you were doing so. There are several dyNAMEic web pages that are database driven, for example. These will take some user input from the forms and clicks that you are doing and use it to create a SQL query. This query will then go through and retrieve information from the database in order to perform the action, such as switching to a new page.

Consider a simple online catalogue that allows you to search to demonstrate how this works. The search page will frequently have a form with only a text box. You can enter the name of the item that you want to search using the form, and then just click on the search button. When you click the search button, the web server will search through the database to locate anything related to that search term. It will return them to create a new web page that corresponds to your specific request.

For those who haven't spent much time learning a programming language and don't consider themselves programmers, the SQL commands aren't too difficult to learn. SQL commands are all written in a syntax that is compatible with the English language.

At first, this will appear to be very complicated, and you may be concerned about how much work it will take to get it set up. However, after you begin working on a few codes, you will see that it is not all that difficult to deal with. Often, simply reading the SQL statement will help you figure out what the command will accomplish. Take a look at the following code:

DELETE

THROUGH STUDENTS

Graduation year = 2014 for WHR

If you read that code aloud, you can probably guess what will happen when you decide to execute it. Most of the SQL code will operate in this manner, so you do not need to be an experienced programmer to make the SQL language work for you. Given that this is a language that allows authorised users to search through a database and retrieve the information they seek, it is easy to see why the SQL language is so popular.

SQL may appear to be a difficult language for you to learn, but it is actually very simple. We will spend some time looking at all of the many things that you can do if you decide to use SQL to help you govern the database that you use in your firm. It is made to be simple and to make things easier when working with databases or when trying to make it simple for your users to discover information, and SQL certainly delivers on this.

HOW DOES THIS WORK WITH YOUR DATABASE?

f you decide that SQL is the language you will use to manage your database, you can look at the database. When you look at this, you will notice that you are essentially just looking at groups of information. Some people will consider these to be organisational mechanisms that will be used to store information that you, the user, can look at later on, and it will do so as efficiently as possible. When it comes to managing your database, SQL may help you with a lot of things, and you will see some great results.

There are times when you are working on a project with your organisation and you may be working with a database that is quite similar to SQL and you may not even realise it. For example, a phone book is a type of database that is regularly used. This will have a wealth of information about people in your area, such as their NAMEe, the type of business they run, their address, and phone numbers. And because all of this information is in one place, you won't have to search all over to discover it.

This is similar to how the SQL database works. It will accomplish this by searching through the information stored in your company's database. It will sort through that information so that you can find what you need faster and without making a mess or losing time.

RATIONALE DATABASE

First, we must examine the relational databases. This database is the one you'll want to use if you want to work with databases that have been aggregated into logical units or other types of tables, and these tables have the ability to be interconnected inside your database in a way that will make sense depending on what you're looking for at the time. These databases can also be useful if you wish to enter some complex information and then use a programme to break it down into smaller pieces so that you can manage it better.

The relational databases are good ones to work with because they allow you to grab on to all the information that you have stored for your business, and then manipulate it in a way that makes it easier to use. You may take that complicated knowledge and simplify it so that you and others can understand it. While you may be perplexed by all of the information and how to break it down, the system will be able to go through it and arrange it the manner you require in no time. You may also get some more security so that if you put personal information about the customer into that database, you can keep it away from others, in other words, it will be completely safe from people who wish to steal it.

TECHNOLOGY OF CLIENT AND SERVER

Now, these systems were able to work, and they got the job done for a long time. If your organisation uses these and this is what you are most comfortable with, it gets the job done. However, there are other alternatives on the market that will perform a better job. These settings are available in the client-server system.

These systems will utlize diferent processes to help you get the results needed. With this one, the main computer that you are using, known as the'server,' will be accessible to any user on the network. Now, these users have to have the request credentials to do this, which helps keep the system safe and secure. However, if the user has the correct information and is connected to your network, they can reach the information with little trouble and effort. The user can get the server from other servers or from their desktop computer, and the user will then be recognised as the 'client' so that the client and server are easily

HOW TO WORK WITH DATABASES THAT ARE AVAILABLE ONLINE

Many business owners will discover that client and server technology is the one that works best for them. This system is great for many companies, but there are some things that you may need to add or remove at times due to how technology has changed recently. Some companies like the idea that their database will perform better with the internet so that they can work on it no matter where they are, whether at home or at the office. There will be times when a customer will have an account with the company and will need to be able to access the database online as well. For example, if you have an Amazon account, you are a member of their database and can acquire access to certain portions through this.

As the trend of companies migrating online continues, it is more typical to see databases moving online as well, and that you must have a website and a solid web browser so that customers can come in and check them out. You can always add user NAMEes and passwords to make it more secure and ensure that only the correct user has access to their information. This is a great way to protect your customers' personal and payment information. Most companies will requre their users to select security credentials to get on the account, but they will offer the account for free.

Of course, this is a simple system to work with, but there will be a number of things going on behind the scenes to ensure that the programme works properly. The customer can simply go onto the system and check the information, but the server will have a lot of work to do to ensure that the information is showing up on the screen correctly, and to ensure that the user has a nice experience and can see their own account information on the screen.

For example, you may be able to see that the web browser you are using uses SQL or a programme similar to it to figure out who the user is that your data is hoping to see. The SQL system will be used to access your database as soon as the customer enters what they are looking for.

WHY IS SQL SO GREAT?

Now that we have spent some time talking about the various types of database management systems that you can work with, it is time to discuss why you would want to choose SQL over some of the other options that are out there. You may deal with other databases as well as different coding languages, and there are advantages to using each one. So, why would you want to deal specifically with SQL? Some of the many benefits of adopting SQL as your database management system include:

Extremely quick

If you want to choose a management system that can quickly sort through information and return results, SQL is one of the best tools to use. Just give it a shot, and you'll be surprised at how much information you can get back and how quickly. In fact, of all the solutions available, this is the most efficient one.

Standards well defined

The database that comes with SQL ha been working well for a long time. Furthermore, it has been able to develop some good standards that ensure the database is strong and functions the way you want it to. Some of the other databases you might want to interact with will not support these standards, which might be frustrating when you use them.

You do not require a lot of coding.

If you're looking at SQL databases, you don't need to be a coding expert to get the job done. We shall look at a few codes that can help, but even a beginner will get them down and do well when working with SQL.

Keeps your belongings organised

When it comes to running your business, it is critical that you can keep your information safe, secure, and organised. And, while there are several great databases to choose from, none will function as well as the SQL language at getting this all done.

DBMS based on Objects

The SQL database relies on the DBMS system that we discussed earlier since it will make it easier to find the information that you are searching for, store the proper items, and perform so much more within the database.

These are only a few of the advantages that you might obtain when you work with the SQL application. While some people struggle with this interface at first, there are a tonne of wonderful features to work on with SQL, and you will really enjoy how fast and easy it is to work with this language and its database.

CHAPITRE 2 LANGUAGE OF DATA DEFINITION

SQL is built around data. After all, SQL was developed to make it easier to manipulate data stored within a database. It ensures that you do not have to manually sort through large amounts of data in search of what you want. Now, depending on the platform used, different types of data can be stored in the database. As a result, you must now learn about the data types available in SQL.

Introduction to Data Types

The data type denotes the type of data that can be stored in a column of a database table. When creating a table, it is critical to decide on the data type that will be used to define the columns. Data types can also be used to define variables and store procedure output and input parameters. The data type instructs SQL to expect a specific type of data in each column.

A data type must be chosen for each variable or column that is appropriate for the type of data that will be stored in that variable or column. Furthermore, storage requirements have to be taken into considered. You must choose data types that will ensure storage efficiency.

Choosing the correct data type for the variables, tables, and stored procedures will greatly improve the performance and ensure that the execution plan is correct. At the same time, there will be a significant improvement in data integrity because it ensures that the correct data is stored within a database.

The Data Types List

SQL employs a number of data types. The table below lists all of them, along with a brief description of what they are. Mark this tab because it will be extremely useful as a reference guide on data types when you are learning and afterwards.

Before you begin, you need take some time to understand what precision and scale are. The total number of digits present in a number is referred to as precision. The scale is the total number of digits located on the right side of a number's decimal point. In the case of a number such as 123.4567, the precision is 7 and the scale is 4.

TIME	Stores hour, minute, and second values
TIMESTAMP	Stores year, month, day, hour, minute, and second values
INTERVAL	Composed of a number of integer fields, representing a period of time, depending on the type of interval
ARRAY	A set-length and ordered collection of elements
MULTISET	A variable-length and unordered collection of elements
XML	Stores XML data

INTEGER (p)	Integer numerical (no decimal). Precision p
SMALLINT	Integer numerical (no decimal). Precision 5
INTEGER	Integer numerical (no decimal). Precision 10
BIGINT	Integer numerical (no decimal). Precision 19
DECIMAL (p,s)	Exact numerical, precision p, scale s. Example: decimal(5,2) is a number that has 3 digits before the decimal and 2 digits after the decimal
NUMERIC (p,s)	Exact numerical, precision p, scale s. (Same as DECIMAL.)
FLOAT(p)	Approximate numerical, mantissa precision p. A floating number in base 10 exponential notation. The size argument for this type consists of a single number specifying the minimum precision
REAL	Approximate numerical, mantissa precision 7
FLOAT	Approximate numerical, mantissa precision 16
DOUBLE PRECISION	Approximate numerical, mantissa precision 16
DATE	Stores year, month, and day values

Differences Between Database Platforms

The data types listed above are shared by all database platforms. However, some are recognised by different NAMEes in different database platforms. This can be a source of consternation. As a result, have a look at the variances in the table below.

Data Type	Access	SQLServer	Oracle	MySQL	PostgreSQL
boolean	Yes/No	Bit	Byte	N/A	Boolean
integer	Number (integer)	Int	Number	Int Integer	Int Integer
float	Number (single)	Float Real	Number	Float	Numeric
currency	Currency	Money	N/A	N/A	Money
string (fixed)	N/A	Char	Char	Char	Char
string (variable)	Text (<256) Memo (65k+)	Varchar	Varchar Varchar 2	Varchar	Varchar
binary object	OLE Object Memo	Binary (fixed up to 8K) Varbinary (<8K) Image (<2GB)	Long Raw	Blob Text	Binary Varbinary

Different Data Types for Different Databases

Each database platform has its own set of data types. As a result, in order to use these platforms effectively, you must first understand what these data types are. We will concentrate on the most popular database systems here: MySQL, SQL Server, and Microsoft Access. With each data type, a brief description has been provided.

Microsoft Access Data Types

MySQL Data Types

Data Type	Description
Text	Use for text or combinations of text and numbers. 255 characters' maximum
Memo	Memo is used for larger amounts of text. Stores up to 65,536 characters. Note: You cannot sort a memo field. However, they are searchable
Byte	Allows whole numbers from 0 to 255. Storage is 1 byte.
Integer	Allows whole numbers between -32,768 and 32,767. Storage is 2 bytes.
Long	Allows whole numbers between -2,147,483,648 and 2,147,483,647. Storage is 4 bytes.
Single	Single precision floating-point. Will handle most decimals. Storage is 4 bytes.
Double	Double precision floating-point. Will handle most decimals. Storage is 8 bytes.
Currency	Use for currency. Holds up to 15 digits of whole dollars, plus 4 decimal places. Tip: You can choose which country's currency to use. Storage is 8 bytes.
AutoNumber	AutoNumber fields automatically give each record its own number, usually starting at 1. Storage is 4 bytes.
Data/Time	Use for dates and times. Storage is 8 bytes.
Yes/No	A logical field can be displayed as Yes/No, True/False, or On/Off. In code, use the constants True and False (equivalent to -1 and 0). Note: Null values are not allowed in Yes/No fields. Storage is 1 bit.
Ole Object	Can store pictures, audio, video, or other BLOBs (Binary Large OBjects). Storage is up to 1GB.
Hyperlink	Contain links to other files, including web pages.
Lookup Wizard	Let you type a list of options, which can then be chosen from a drop-down list. Storage is 4 bytes

The data types available in MySQL can be broadly classified into three categories. They are text, date/temperate, and number. We will examine the available data types in each category in the next tables.

Data Type (Text)	Description
CHAR(size)	Holds a fixed length string (can contain letters, numbers, and special characters). The fixed size is specified in parenthesis. Can store up to 255 characters.
VARCHAR(size)	Holds a variable length string (can contain letters, numbers, and special characters). The maximum size is specified in parenthesis. Can store up to 255 characters. Note: If you put a greater value than 255 it will be converted to a TEXT type
TINYTEXT	Holds a string with a maximum length of 255 characters
TEXT	Holds a string with a maximum length of 65,535 characters
BLOB	For BLOBs (Binary Large OBjects). Holds up to 65,535 bytes of data
MEDIUMTEXT	Holds a string with a maximum length of 16,777,215 characters
MEDIUMBLOB	For BLOBs (Binary Large OBjects). Holds up to 16,777,215 bytes of data
LONGTEXT	Holds a string with a maximum length of 4,294,067,295 characters
LONGBLOB	For BLOBs (Binary Large OBjects). Holds up to 4,294,067,295 bytes of data
ENUM(x,y,z,etc.)	Let you enter a list of possible values. You can list up to 65535 values in an ENUM list. If a value is inserted that is not in the list, a blank value will be inserted. Note: The values are sorted in the order you enter them. You enter the possible values in this format: ENUM(X,Y,Z)
SET	Similar to ENUM except that SET may contain up to 64 list items and can store more than one choice

Types of MySQL Data

Integers:

In MySQL, integrated data types will have an additional option known as UNSIGND. In general, an integrer will shift from a negative value to a positive one. However, the insertion of the UNSIGND attribute will raise that ange. As a result, the integrer will begin with zero rather than a negative number.

Data Type (Number)	Description
TINYINT(size)	-128 to 127 normal. 0 to 255 UNSIGNED*. The maximum number of digits may be specified in parenthesis
SMALLINT(size)	-32768 to 32767 normal. 0 to 65535 UNSIGNED*. The maximum number of digits may be specified in parenthesis
MEDIUMINT(size)	-8388608 to 8388607 normal. 0 to 16777215 UNSIGNED*. The maximum number of digits may be specified in parenthesis
INT(size)	-2147483648 to 2147483647 normal. 0 to 4294967295 UNSIGNED*. The maximum number of digits may be specified in parenthesis
BIGINT(size)	-9223372036854775808 to 9223372036854775807 normal. 0 to 18446744073709551615 UNSIGNED*. The maximum number of digits may be specified in parenthesis
FLOAT(size,d)	A small number with a floating decimal point. The maximum number of digits may be specified in the size parameter. The maximum number of digits to the right of the decimal point is specified in the d parameter
DOUBLE(size,d)	A large number with a floating decimal point. The maximum number of digits may be specified in the size parameter. The maximum number of digits to the right of the decimal point is specified in the d parameter
DECIMAL(size,d)	A DOUBLE stored as a string, allowing for a fixed decimal point. The maximum number of digits may be specified in the size parameter. The maximum number of digits to the right of the decimal point is specified in the d parameter

Date/Time:

The two data types, TIMSTAMP and DATTIM, can both return the same format. They do, however, work in different ways. TIMSTAMP will automatically set itself to the current time and date in a UPDAT or INSRT query. Different forms are also accepted by TIMSTAMP.

Data Type (Date)	Description
DATE()	A date. Format: YYYY-MM-DD Note: The supported range is from '1000-01-01' to '9999-12-31'
DATETIME()	*A date and time combination. Format: YYYY-MM-DD HH:MI:SS Note: The supported range is from '1000-01-01 00:00:00' to '9999-12-31 23:59:59'
TIMESTAMP()	*A timestamp. TIMESTAMP values are stored as the number of seconds since the Unix epoch ('1970-01-01 00:00:00' UTC). Format: YYYY-MM-DD HH:MI:SS Note: The supported range is from '1970-01-01 00:00:01' UTC to '2038-01-09 03:14:07' UTC
TIME()	A time. Format: HH:MI:SS Note: The supported range is from '-838:59:59' to '838:59:59'
YEAR()	A year in two-digit or four-digit format. Note: Values allowed in four-digit format: 1901 to 2155. Values allowed in two-digit format: 70 to 69, representing years from 1970 to 2069

SQL Server Data Types

Like MySQL, the data types in SQL Server can be classified into various categories. We'll take a look at each of the tables below.

String:

Data Type (String)	Description	Storage
char(n)	Fixed width character string. Maximum 8,000 characters	Defined width
varchar(n)	Variable width character string. Maximum 8,000 characters	2 bytes + number of chars
varchar(max)	Variable width character string. Maximum 1,073,741,824 characters	2 bytes + number of chars
text	Variable width character string. Maximum 2GB of text data	4 bytes + number of chars
nchar	Fixed width Unicode string. Maximum 4,000 characters	Defined width x 2
nvarchar	Variable width Unicode string. Maximum 4,000 characters	
nvarchar(max)	Variable width Unicode string. Maximum 536,870,912 characters	
ntext	Variable width Unicode string. Maximum 2GB of text data	
bit	Allows 0, 1, or NULL	
binary(n)	Fixed width binary string. Maximum 8,000 bytes	
varbinary	Variable width binary string. Maximum 8,000 bytes	
varbinary(max)	Variable width binary string. Maximum 2GB	
image	Variable width binary string. Maximum 2GB	

<u>**Number:**</u>

Data Type (Number)	Description	Storage
tinyint	Allows whole numbers from 0 to 255	Stores up to 1 byte
smallint	Allows whole numbers between -32,768 and 32,767	Stores up to 2 bytes
int	Allows whole numbers between -2,147,483,648 and 2,147,483,647	Stores up to 4 bytes
bigint	Allows whole numbers between -9,223,372,036,854,775,808 and 9,223,372,036,854,775,807	Stores up to 8 bytes
decimal(p,s)	Fixed precision and scale numbers. Allows numbers from -10^38 +1 to 10^38 -1. The p parameter indicates the maximum total number of digits that can be stored (both to the left and to the right of the decimal point). p must be a value from 1 to 38. Default is 18. The s parameter indicates the maximum number of digits stored to the right of the decimal point. s must be a value from 0 to p. Default value is 0	Stores between 5-17 bytes

<u>**Date/Time**</u>:

The preceding tables will certainly be of immense help in your work. You should unquestionably go.

Data Type (Date)	Description	Storage
datetime	From January 1, 1753 to December 31, 9999 with an accuracy of 3-33 milliseconds	Stores up to 8 bytes
datetime2	From January 1, 0001 to December 31, 9999 with an accuracy of 100 nanoseconds	Stores between 6-8 bytes
smalldatetime	From January 1, 1900 to June 6, 2079 with an accuracy of 1 minute	Stores up to 4 bytes
date	Store a date only. From January 1, 0001 to December 31, 9999	Stores up to 3 bytes
time	Store a time only to an accuracy of 100 nanoseconds	Stores between 3-5 bytes
datetimeoffset	The same as datetime2 with the addition of a time zone offset	Stores between 8-10 bytes
timestamp	Stores a unique number that gets updated every time a row gets created or modified. The timestamp value is based upon an internal clock and does not correspond to real time. Each table may have only one timestamp variable.	

over them more than once to ensure that you have a solid understanding of the data types in use in SQL in various database platforms. In fact, marking down the chapter will be a smart idea so that you can immediately refer to it whenever you need to refresh your knowledge.

THE DIFFERENT TYPES OF DATA THAT WORK IN SQL

Now that we've looked at some of the commands that you'll want to use outside of the SQL language, it's time to look at some of the data types that you can use to make this SQL language perform well when you're creating your new code. These data types will change depending on what you want to have done within that database as well as the various items that you want to offer or sell to your customers.

The various data types that are most commonly found inside of this SQL system will be the attributes that will go with the information that is on the inside, and these specific characteristics will be placed on a table that you can read through and retrieve any time that you would like to have a look.

Let's look at how this works. A suitable example is when you require that a field you want to deal with can only hold numeric valeues. You will discover that you can use SQL to set it all up such that the user can only place a number within that database, or at least in that specific cell of the table. So, if you have a cell on the table where you only want them to put their phone number or credit card number, you may add this as a restriction. By assigning the proper types of data to the fields that you want to see inside the table, you ensure that fewer errors appear on the customer's side.

One thing to keep in mind while working with your SQL system is that all of the versions that you can work with will be slightly different, and you may have to make some different choices when selecting the data that you want to use. You must review the rules that come with the version of SQL you are using to ensure that everything stays in order. In most cases, you can use the data points that are specific to the version that you choose to ensure that the database is working properly.

There are some basic types of data that you can use when dealing with SQL regardless of which version you are using. Some of the data types that you can use are:

- Time and date values
- Numeric strings
- Character strings

CHARACTERS WHICH ARE FIXED IN LENGTH

Now it's time to look at some of the many types of data that you can interact with outside of SQL. The fixed length character is the first one you might want to use. If you wish to deal with consistent characters or strings that stay the same all the time, you must ensure that they are saved correctly in the system. The typical data type that you will want to work with when selecting these characters is as follows:

Character(n)

Examine the example above carefully; the 'n' that we placed inside the parenthesis is the maximum length or the assigned length that you will allow that particular field to be. You can use this for the phone number field, for example. You'd want to keep it at ten characters so that the customer only enters a phone number and nothing else. You may also do this for some of the other parts of the code, but you'll have to be careful. For example, if you impose these restrictions on the customer's name, they may have some difficulties if their name is longer than the characters that you permit.

Depending on the version of SQL, you may discover that it will function with the 'CHAR' data type instead, to save information of a fixed length. Working with this type of data is an excellent idea if you want to work with any alphanumeric information. So, if you want to set up a portion that will allow the user to place in their NAMEe of their state, but you want to make sure that they use the abbreviation of the state rather than the whole NAMEe, you can use the character limit and set it to two so that everyone knows how it should operate.

When working with the character of the data type, your user will not enter information that is longer than the character limit that you set. Let's assume you live in South Dakota, but you want to make sure that the user may only enter the abbreviation for two characters. If the user tries to enter more than two characters at this point, it will not work.

There are many times when working with your database that you will wish to limit the characters that you and the user can use. However, while working with the password and userNAMEe that your user should be allowed to use, it is best not to use a fixed character length for these. Allow the user to choose what is best for this. Sometimes you may want to set a minimum length to help with security, but never set a maximum so that the user has the freedom they require to create a decent userNAMEe and password.

DISTINCTIVE CHARACTERS

It is also possible to deal with variable characters rather than the fixed length characters discussed above. Instead of telling the user how many characters they are allowed to have, you can let them choose how lengthy this should be. This is a wonderful option if you're working with fields like the NAMEe (which may easily reach various lengths depending on the person) as well as userNAMEes or passwords that the user would like to use to make them unique. If you have a field that you would like to use in this manner, the notation that you would use is as follows:

Variable character (n)

With the option that we used above, you will notice that the 'n' will be the number that identifies the maximum or the assigned value. You will then be able to choose from a variety of different types that you would like to put in here to work with your variable characters such as ANSI, VARCHAR, or VARCHAR2.

For this particular data type, there are no requirements that you must meet when filling up the spaces for your user. If you assigned a length of 15 characters, the user would be able to add in some less if they wanted, and you would not have issues as you would with the fixed length characters we discussed before.

If you are interested in working with some character strings that may be considered variables in your language, you should use varied data types as much as possible. The reason for this is that it will help you to maximise the amount of space that you can use in your database and will make it easier for the user to submit their information without confounding the database in the process.

NUMERIC VALUE

Now we'll look at how these numeric values can be used in your code with SQL. When you are in the SQL system, you can work with numeric values whenever you want. These are the values that you will store in the field utilising a number rather than a letter. These values will have diferent NAMEes depending on which numeric value you choose to use in your code. However, there are several that are more common to work with, and these are as follows:

- Integer
- Double precision
- Bit varying (n)
- Real
- Float
- Decimal
- Bit

LITERAL STRINGS IN DECIMALS

Another item you may look at and work with while working with SQL is 'literal strings.'

These will be a series of characters, such as a list of NAMEes and phone numbers, specified by the user or the database. For the most part, you will see that these strings will store a large amount of data with comparable characteristics.

When working with literal strings, it is sometimes difficult to specify what type of data you want to use. As a result, you will spend time specifying the type of string you wish to use to ensure that everything works. It is important to understand that when you work to create these strings, especially if the string will end up being alphanumeric, you must ensure that these are quotes that may go throughout the world. You can use either single or double quotation marks on this one; just make sure they are the same on both sides of the word to help the compiler out.

BOOLAN VALUES

You can also operate with what are known as Boolean values. These Boolean values are crucial because they will perform a variety of different functions within the SQL system, making it easier to work on some of the searches that you want to undertake. When working with Boolean values, there are three alternatives that will appear. True, false, and null are the three alternatives.

When working with the Boolean values, you will discover that employing these values can be helpful when you wish to compare several units of data outside of your table. You would be able to use these units to determine whether they are matching or not, and you would then receive the correct answer based on the Boolean values. For example, you might use this in SQL to specify the parameters of a search, and all of the criteria that come back to you will either be true, false, or null depending on what you're comparing.

With these kinds of values, you should keep in mind that it will only provide you the results if the answer is correct. If the answer to these values is null or false, the data will not be retrieved from the database for you or the user. However, if you end up with a true value, you will see that all of the information is true and will show up for you.

When your user is in the database and wants to do a search to discover something, this is a nice method to look at it. If the product's keywords match what the user is typing into the search bar, then true answers will appear, while everything else will remain hidden.

If you have your own website and sell products online, you will spend a lot of time working with these Boolean values. These values will ensure that you get the proper results from your software. So, if the user goes through and types in a keyword that they want to be able to locate outside of the code, the Boolean value will be able to look at that and find the results that fit in.

Don't worry if this sounds complicated; the SQL system is capable of assisting you in getting this done in a simple manner so that your customers can find what they want without having to fret or struggle with the website.

There are many different applications where you can use some of the Boolean expressions in SQL, but as a beginner, this is likely to be the method you will use the most. You can also use it while searching through your database for specific answers to questions, or when searching through the store or programme for specific information. When you enter some of this information into SQL tables, you can speed up the process more than ever before.

It is critical to remember how these Boolean results will work. They are in charge of determining whether something corresponds to what you are looking for. If something matches the keywords that you enter into the system, it will appear. However, if other objects or items do not match up with this, they will be displayed as false or null and will not appear.

Assume you're using a website to sell some of your products, such as apparel. Someone visits your website and wants to find dresses for special occasions. If they type the word 'dress' into the search field, you want to make sure they see the things they want rather than something else. This means that dresses should appear on the screen after the search is completed rather than shoes or accessories.

This will happen if the Boolean values are used. If the user enters 'dress' into the system, the Boolean value will go over each item and check to see if they are true to this statement. If the item contains the word 'dress,' it will appear on your screen. If the item lacks that keyword, the Boolean value will see it as a false statement and will not display it on the screen. As long as the Boolean value is functioning properly, your user will be able to obtain the items they desire, and only those items will appear on the screen.

This can be quite useful for anyone who is selling products on the internet, especially if they have a large inventory to choose from and need a software such as SQL, to sort through a tonne of data to figure it out. The Boolean values will do all of the work for you to help prevent problems.

As you can see from this chapter, there are various data types that you may deal with besides SQL to make your searches and programme easier and simpler. Each data type will work differently so that you get the proper results and get more than you need.

CHAPTER 3. WHAT IS DATA DESCRIPTION LANGUAGE?

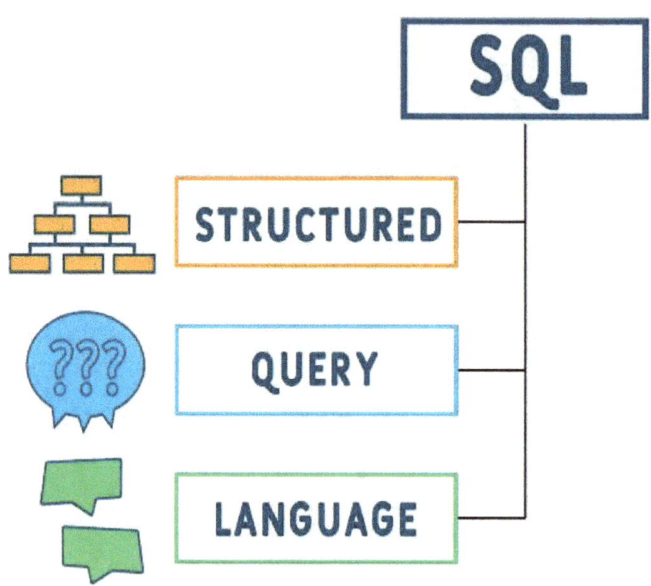

Now that we've spent some time learning what SQL is all about, as well as some of the fundamentals of the databases that business owners will use, it's time to learn more about this system. This chapter will require some time to learn some of the commands that you will need to use to ensure that you get this system to accomplish what you want.

Do not be concerned if this sounds frightening at first. This is a simple language to learn, and the commands are simple to use. It is not nearly as complicated as some of the other coding languages with which you may like to work. This chapter will assist you with these commands by categorising them into six categories so that you understand how each one works. The six types of commands that you will use when dealing with SQL are as follows:

<u>LANGUAGE OF DATA DEFINITION</u>

This category is known as the 'DDL,' and it is one of the aspects of SQL that you must learn. This is in charge of allowing you to generate objects into the database before arranging them in the best method for you. For example, this is the aspect of the SQL system that you should use any time you want to make changes to your table, such as adding or removing objects. There are some commands that you may use to help you see these changes. These are some examples:

- Create a table
- Alter a table
- Drop a table
- Create an index
- Alter an index
- Drop view
- Drop index

<u>LANGUAGE FOR DATA MANIPULATION</u>

The next item you can work with outside of SQL is data manipulation language. When working with SQL, this is referred to as 'DML,' and it is the part that you can use to edit the objects that are outside of your database. This allows your users and you to have more freedom when browsing through the information in your database and allows you to contribute something new that will help the database perform better.

LANGUAGE OF DATA QUERY

When you work with the data query language, also known as 'DQL,' you will be working with what many experts consider to be the most powerful aspect of the SQL system. If you want to work with the DQL outside of this software, you simply need one command to get it to function. The command that you will need to use to make this work is 'Select.' This is a easy command to work with that will provide you a variety of options, including running queries while you are within your relational database. If you want to get more detailed results, make sure you're using the select command in DQL.

LANGUAGE FOR DATA CONTROL

Another aspect of SQL that you should learn is how to use the data control language if you want to add more power to the code that you are writing. This will work well if you want to have more control over who has access to the database. If your organisation deals with your customers' personal information, such as credit card information, it is a good idea to use data control language so that you may set certain boundaries on who can use these databases and access the information.

The DCL command will be used to help generate the objects that you need to control who has access to the information in the database so that only the right people may get into the database. You may restrict who can access the database, who can distribute the information in the database, and much more.

Some of the commands that you would be able to use outside of the DCL are as follows:

Revoke

Grand

Alternative password

Create a synonym

DATA ADMINISTRATION OPTIONS

When you are working with some commands that operate well within the SQL system, you can also find a few that can analyze and audit the operation that is within the database. There are also times when you can access the performance on the database overall with the help of these same commands. If you want to fix something inside the database that isn't operating properly, or if you want to make sure you get rid of issues that are affecting the system, you can use these instructions. While there are several possibilities available to you, the two that you are most likely to work with are:

Audit Begin

Audit End

One thing to keep in mind when working with the SQL system is that the database administrator and the data administrator are two distinct roles. So, the database administrator is the component of the code that will manage all of the parts of your database, such as the commands you are setting up outside of SQL, and these commands will be more specific in their implementation in SQL.

COMMANDS FOR TRANSACTIONAL CONTROL

There may be many occasions when you will want to manage and keep track of transactions that are outside of your database. If you are attempting to perform this within a database, you should use transactional control instructions to make it work. If you have your own website to sell your product, you will find that these commands will help you keep it all in line. These transactional control commands can be used for a variety of purposes, including:

- **Commit**

This is the command to use if you want to save information relating to the various transactions that appear in the database.

- **Savepoint**

You should use this command if you want to generate different points inside a collection of transactions. You should also use this command at the same time as the rollback command, which we shall discuss later.

- **Command to Roll Back**

The rollback command is the one you will use when you want to browse through your database and see which ones you can undo inside.

* **Set up transactions**

This is the command to use any time you want to enter your transactions into the database and give them NAMEes. The first transaction will be the one you use if you want to try to label things for a bit more organisation.

When working outside of SQL, it is critical to learn how to work with all six of these categories. They will assist you in getting more out of your searches so that the database will provide you with the information you are looking for. We'll spend some time exploring these as we move through this guidebook so you can use them a little bit better. Understanding some of the fundamentals that come with your SQL system can help you get the best results while using this system.

CHAPTERS 4. LEARN MORE ABOUT ADDING, REMOVING, AND UPDATING DATA.

FORMULATING A DATABASE

To create a new database in SQL, we use the CRAT DATABAS command. The command uses the syntax given below:

CREAT DATABAS DatabaseNAMEe;

Assume we need to create a database called Company1. We can run the following command:

Company1 CREAT DATABAS;

The database should be successfully created.

Now that the database has been created, you can use the SHOW DATABASS command to see if the process was successful:

DISPLAY DATABASES;

You can see that Company1 is listed among the databases that we have, indicating that the database was successfully created.

IF DOES NOT EXIST

SQL server supports many databases. You may not be the only person who has access to the SQL server. In such a case, you could try to create a database that already exists. The IF NOT EXISTS clause allows you to check for the existence of a database with a comparable name before creating one

The database will only be created if the specified database does not already exist. No changes will occur if the database exists. If you try to recreate an already existing database without using the IF NOT XISTS clause, MySQL will throw an error. Let us try to recreate the Company1 database:

Company1 CREAT DATABASE;

As demonstrated above, the command returns a error. Let us demonstrate the use of the IF NOT XISTS clause:

CREAT DATABASE IF COMPANY1 DOES NOT EXIST;

As seen above, this returns no error. However, no changes will be made to the existing database.

CREATIVE TABLES

The creation of a table entails defining the table NAMEe and its columns. Each column's data types must also be defined. The CRAT TABL command is used to create the table.

The syntax demonstrates that the CRAT TABL command is followed by the NAMEe of the table to be created, followed by the columns. Using the PRIMARY KY keyword, you can specify the column to be the primary key.

However, before you can create the table, you must first select the datable in which you want to create the table. It should be noted that a table is created in a database. The US command is used to select the database. In our case, we must create the table within the Company1 database. We can select the database by issuing the following command:

USE Corporation 1;

The database has been chosen. Let us now make the table:

The table has been successfully created. The NOT NULL parameter indicates that the column must have a value, which means that the ID column must have a value for each entry made into the table.

We can use the DSC command to see the table's details. It is an abbreviation for DSCRIB, and it is followed by the NAMEe of the table:

DSC EMPLOYERS;

The preceding demonstrates that the table was successfully created.

IF DOES NOT EXIST

This clause assists us in creating the table if one does not already exist. If the table is already in the database, it will not be created. Let us attempt to re-create a table that already exists. We already have the MPLOYS table. Let us re-create it without this clause:

CREATE TABLE EMPLOYEES(

 ID INT NOT NULL,

NAMEE VARCHAR (15) NOT NULL,

ADDRESS CHAR (20) ,

AGE INT NOT NULL,

SALARY DECIMAL (16, 2),

PRIMARY KEY (ID);

The command returns a error saying that the table already exists. To prevent getting an error if the table already exists, we can use the IF NOT XISTS lause, as seen below:

CREATE TABLE IF NOT

EXISTS EMPLOYEES(

ID INT NOT NULL,

NAMEE VARCHAR (15) NOT NULL,

ADDRESS CHAR (20) ,

AGE INT NOT NULL,

SALARY DECIMAL (16, 2),

PRIMARY KEY (ID)

The command will produce the following results:

The command returns no error this time.

DATA INSTRUCTION

The goal of database systems is to store data in tables. This information is supplemented by application programmes that run on top of the database. The NSRT statement in SQL allows us to enter data into a table for storage. The command adds a new row to the table.

The syntax of the command is as follows:

INSERT INTO tableNAMEe (column 1,column 2,...) VALUS (value1 value2,...);

Note that we have specified the NAMEe of the table to insert data into, the NAMEes of the columns into which we need to insert the data, the data vale that are to be inserted, and the data vales that are to be inserted If you need to insert data into all of the table's columns, you don't need to specify the column NAMEes. However, if you need to insert data into some columns while skipping others, specify which columns you need to insert data into.

The following command explains how to insert data into all of the table' columns:

INSERT INTO EMPLOYS VALUE (1, 'jOHN,' 'John12,' 26, 3000.00);

The command was executed successfully, as seen above. This indicates that row has been created in the table.

However, you may simply need to insert data into a few columns. This is th time to specify the NAMEes of the columns into which you will insert th data.

Assume we don't know the employee's salary. We can insert data into th following columns:

INESRT INTO EMPLOYS (ID, NAME, ADDRESS, AG) VALUS (2 'Mercy,' 'Mercy32,' 25);

The preceding command had no effect on the salary column.

<u>DATA FOR VIEWING TABLE</u>

A database's job is to store data that can be retrieved. The data is retrieved by using the SELECTT command.

The command's syntax is as follows:

SELECT column 1, column 2,..., column N FROM tableNAMEe

The column 1, column 2,..., column N denote the NAMEes of the columns for the table whose values we need to view.

If you need to see data from all of the table columns/fields, use the following command syntax:

SELECT * FROM tableNAMEE;

So far, our MPLOYS have the following data:

Assume we need to see the ID, NAME, and SALARY.

columns. We can execute the following command:

SELECT ID, NAME, AND SALARY FROM MPLOYS;

The command only returns data from the three specified columns.

If we need to query data from all columns/fields, we can use the following command:

* SELECT * FROM MPLOYS;

The command returns data from all of the table's columns.

WHERE Clause

This clause assists us in identifying a condition while we are fetching data from a single or several tables. When the clause is used, only the data that meets the specified criteria is returned. The clause should be ued when you need to filter the records and fetch only the requered records.

It should be noted that the WHR clause is not just used with the SELECTT statement, but it may also be used with other SQL statements. When using it with the SELECTT statement, use the syntax given below:

SELECT column 1, SELECT column 2, SELECT column N

WHERE [condition] FROM tableNAMEe

There are a number of comparative operators you can use to specify the condition. xemples include

>, =, NOT, LIKE, and so on.

Assume we need to select all rows from the table MPLOYS where the AG of the employees is present.

25. We can execute the following command:

*SELECTT *

FROM EMPLOY'S WHR AG = 25;

This yields the following results:

Only one row has a value of AG equal to 25.

If we need the NAMEes of all employees whose SALARY is greater than $1,000, we can use the following command:

SELECT NAMEE FROM EMPLOYS

WHERE SALARY ABOVE 1000;

Only one employee earns more than $1,000 per month.

Assume we need to see the details of the employee by the name "Mercy," we can execute the following command:

*SELECT *

FROM EMPLOY'S WHR NAME = "MRCY"

This yields the following result:

CONJUNCTIVE OPERATING SYSTEMS

When querying the database, the conjunctive operators help us in combining many conditions. They allow us to perform several comparisons with different operators in a single SQL statement. We will be discussing the AND and OR operators, which are conjunctive operators in SQL.

- **AND OPERATING SYSTEM**

This operator is used in the WHR clause to specify several conditions. When used with the WHR clause, it should adhere to the syntax outlined below:

FROM tableNAMEe SELECTCT column 1, column 2,..., column N

WHERE [condition 1], [condition 2],..., [condition N];

The AND operator allows you to combine N number of conditions. All of the conditions joined by the AND operator must be TRUE for the SQL statement to return the results.

Assume the EMPLOYS table contains the following information:

Assume we need to see the details of all employees under the age of 30.

If their SALARY is greater than $2500, we can use the following command:

*SELECT *

APPROVED BY EMPLOYS

WHR age 30 AND SALARY ABOVE $2500;

The command yields two records. The two records meet both of the conditions specified in the WHR clause.

- ## **OR OPERATING SYSTEM**

This operator also allows us to combine a number of SQL criteria in the WHR clause. The operator uses the syntax given below:

FROM tableNAMEe SELECT column 1, column 2, column N

WHR [condition 1] OR [condition 2] OR [condition N]

It's worth noting that you can use the OR operator to combine multiple conditions. To return results, at least one of the conditions joined by the OR operator must be true.

We will use our MPLOYS table with the following information:

Assume we need to see the NAMEes, ages, and salaries of the employees whose AG is equal to ours.

equal to or greater than 30 or their SALARY is equal to or greater than 3000

We run the following command:

SELECTT NAME, AG, SALARY FROM MPLOYS

WHR age = 30 OR SALARY ABOVE 3000;

The conditions were met by 5 records. It should be noted that the record just needs to meet one of the conditions rather than both.

- ## **RECORDS FOR DELETING**

You may need to delete some records from your table at times. The DELETE clause can be used to accomplish this successfully.

f you simply need to delete a few specific records from your table, combine

1e DELETE and WHR clauses. Alternatively, all table records will be

eleted.

he DELETE command uses the syntax given below:

)ELETE FROM tabelNAMEe WHR [condition];

f you have a lot of conditions, combine them with AND or OR clauses.

)ur EMPLOYS table contains the following information:

et us remove the employee with the NAMEe "jOHN" from the table:

)elete from mployee WHR NAME = "jOHN";

ou can then use the SELECTT command to determine whether or not the

cord was successfully deleted.

he good thing about SQL is that it is not case sensitive, which means that the

eletion would have been successful even if you typed the NAMEe in a case

1at did not match the way it is stored in the database.

your goal is to delete all of the records in the table, you do not need to

ombine the DELETE statement with the WHR clause. You only need to run

1e following command:

DELETE * FROM EMPLOYS;

he command will delete all of the records in the table EMPLOYEES

CHAPTERS 5. HOW TO SECURE DATA FROM SQL TABLES

The SELECT key can be used to choose a datum from your database. You only need to select the data you wish to select.

Step 1–Select the SELECT statement

Select SELECTT to identify your SQL command.

Step 2– Select a column

Choose the specific column from which you wish to retrieve the data.

Example: SELECT"column NAMEe"

Step 3–Utilize the asterisk * to select all columns.

If you want to choose all columns, use *; otherwise, you can select as many columns as you want.

Example: SELECT"column NAMEe1"

[–eolumn NAMEe2",–eolumn NAMEe3"]

Step #4–Insert FROM and the NAMEe of the table from which the dat will be retrieved.

You can use open and close square brackets [] to enclose the identifie columns and where conditions, but this is optional.

Example: SELECT"column NAMEe"

["column NAMEe","column NAMEe"] FROM "tabl NAMEe"

WEHRE "column NAMEe";

You can alternatively write the preceding example in this manner:

Example: select column NAMEe, column NAMEe,

from table NAMEe.

Where column NAMEe;

Step #5–Clarify the "CONDITION"

The common operators presented in chapter 4 might be used to specify the condition.

Example #1: SELECT"column NAMEe"

["column NAMEe","column NAMEe"] FROM 'table NAMEe" [where"column NAMEe" "condition"];

You may alternatively write the above example in this manner: (no open and close square brackets)

Exemple #2: select column NAMEe, column NAMEe, column NAMEe from table NAMEe

condition where column NAMEe;

Example #3: SELECT"column NAMEe"

,"column NAMEe", "column NAMEe"] DERIVED FROM "tabl NAMEe"

WHR "column NAMEe"LIK'Am']

In the preceding example, all entries that begin or match with'Am' will be displayed.

Example: SELECT"column NAMEe"

DERIVED FROM "table NAMEe"

WHR "column NAMEe"="America";

Only the rows that exactly match or equal 'America' will be selected in the preceding example.

Reminder:

When utilising the actual NAMEes of the tables and columns, you can remove the double quotes.

SQL QUERIES SAMPLE

Before we go any further, let's do some exercises for simple SQL queries. A sample table is provided below to serve as your practise table.

Traffic hs_2064 sample table

Traffic hs_2064

Country	Searchword	Time (minutes)	Post
America	perfect	5	Matchmaker
Italy	partner	2	NatureTripping
Sweden	mate	10	Fiction
Spain	couple	3	News

Malaysia	team	6	Health
Philippines	island	5	Entertainment
Africa	lover	4	Opinion

Construct or create your SQL statements, syntax, or queries from the following instances using the table above.

1. Retrieve only the country, time, and postcode.

2. Retrieve the nation, searchword, and post.

3. Retrieve all columns for every country with a time less than 5 minutes.

4. Retrieve all columns for every country with a time greater than 6 minutes.

5. Retrieve all columns for each nation that contains the word 'America.'

6. Retrieve all files.

7. Retrieve all columns for any country that isn't 'America.'

8. Retrieve only the searchword and the post.

9. Retrieve only the country and postcode.

10. Retrieve all columns for each country whose NAMEe equals 'Italy.'

Before looking at the answers, try completing the exercises listed above on your computer. You can also use a pencil and paper to tweak your answers if you feel more at ease with this method.

Remember that your SQL command or key words (SELECTT, DELETE, DROP TABL, and similar statements) are not case sensitive, therefore you can use either the lower or upper case.

Column NAMEes and table NAMEes are not case sensitive in Microsoft, but table NAMEes are in UNIX. You must keep track of the database software you are employing.

When you get the data, the results of your SQL query should be displayed on your monitor.

There are answers; SQL statements and resultng tables (outputs)

1.SQL statement:

SELECT country, time, post FROM traffic_hs2064;

Resulting table

Traffic_hs2064

Country	Time (minutes)	Post
America	5	Matchmaker
Italy	2	NatureTripping
Sweden	10	Fiction

Spain	3	News
Malaysia	6	Health
Philippines	5	Entertainment
Africa	4	Opinion

. SQL statement:

ELECT country, searchword, post FROM traffic_hs2064;

Resulting table

Traffic_hs2064

Country	Searchword	Post
America	perfect	Matchmaker
Italy	partner	NatureTripping
Sweden	mate	Fiction
Spain	couple	News

Malaysia	team	Health
Philippines	island	Entertainment
Africa	lover	Opinion

3. SQL statement:

SELECT country, searchword, time, post FROM traffic_hs206◂

where time < 5;

or you could also state it this way:

SELECT * from traffic_hs2064 where time < 5;**Resulting table**

Traffic_hs2064

Country	Searchword	Time (minutes)	Post
Italy	partner	2	NatureTripping
Spain	couple	3	News

| Africa | lover | 4 | Opinion |

4. SQL statement:

SELECT country, searchword, time, post FROM traffic_hs

WHERE time > 6;

or you could also express it this way:

SELECT * FROM traffic_hs2064 WHERE time > 6;

Resulting table

Traffic_hs2064

Country	Searchword	Time (minutes)	Post
Sweden	mate	10	Fiction

5. SQL statement:

SELECT * FROM traffic_hs2064WHEREcountry _America';

Resulting table

Traffic_hs2064

Country	Searchword	Time	Post

		(minutes)	
America	perfect	5	Matchmaker

6. SQL statement:

SELECT * FROM traffic_hs2064

Resulting table

Traffic_hs2064

Country	Searchword	Time (minutes)	Post
America	perfect	5	Matchmaker
Italy	partner	2	NatureTripping
Sweden	mate	10	Fiction
Spain	couple	3	News
Malaysia	team	6	Health

Philippines	island	5	Entertainment
Africa	lover	4	Opinion

7. SQL statement:

SELECT * FROM traffic_hs2064 WHEREcountry < > America';

Resulting table

Traffic_hs2064

Country	Searchword	Time (minutes)	Post
Italy	partner	2	Nature Tripping
Sweden	mate	10	Fiction
Spain	couple	3	News
Malaysia	team	6	Health

Philippines	island	5	Entertainment
Africa	lover	4	Opinion

8. SQL statement:

SELECT searchword, post FROM traffic_hs2064;

Resulting table

Traffic_hs2064

Searchword	Post
perfect	Matchmaker
partner	NatureTripping
mate	Fiction
couple	News
team	Health

island	Entertainment
lover	Opinion

. SQL statement:

ELECT country, post FROM traffic_hs2064;

Resulting table

Traffic_hs2064

Country	Post
America	Matchmaker
Italy	NatureTripping
Sweden	Fiction
Spain	News
Malaysia	Health

Philippines	Entertainment
Africa	Opinion

10. SQL statement:

SELECT * FROM traffic_hs2064 WHEREcountry =_Italy';

Resulting table

Traffic_hs2064

Country	Searchword	Time (minutes)	Post
Italy	partner	2	NatureTripping

These are basic SQL statements or queries that you must know before you ca
proceed to more complex forms.

Practice more with your own SQL software. Of course, by now, you should hav
downloaded an SQL program in your computer. Windows'MySQL program an
Microsoft SQL server are more preferable for beginners

COMBINING AND JOINING TABLES

There will be times that you have to combine tables. This task can be more comple
than simply creating tables. But like everything that you do, the difficulty is all in yo
mind. If you think you can, then you can. So, here goes.

The steps in combining tables are the following:

Step #1– SELECT the columns you want to combine

You can indicate this with the SQL key word SELECT. This will display the columns you want to combine.

Example: SELECT"column_NAMEe","colum_NAMEe"FROM "table_NAMEe"

Step #2– Add the keyword UNION

Add the key word UNION to indicate your intent of combining the tables.

Example: SELECT"column_NAMEe","column_NAMEe"from"table_NAMEe" UNION

Step #3–SELECT the other columns

Now, SELECT the other columns you want to combine with your first selected columns.

Example: SELECT"column_NAMEe","column_NAMEe" FROM "table_NAMEe"

UNION SELECT"column_NAMEe","column_NAMEe"FROM "table_NAMEe";

Step #4–Use UNION ALL, in some cases

You can proceed to this step, in cases, when you want to include duplicate data. Without the key word"ALL",duplicate data would automatically be deleted.

Example: SELECT"column_NAMEe","column_NAMEe"FROM "table_NAMEe"

UNION ALL SELECT"column_NAMEe","column_NAMEe"FROM "table_NAMEe";

Combining tables with the SQL statement SELECT and JOIN

When your database server cannot handle the heavy load of your SELECT UNION query, you could also use the keyword JOIN.

The same steps apply for these statements. All you have to do is add the appropriate JOIN keyw

There are many types of JOIN SQL queries. These are:

INNER JOIN (SIMPLE JOIN) – This will return or retrieve all data from tables that are joined. However, columns will not be displayed when one of the joined tables has no data.

Example: SELECT ̶column1",̶column2" FROM ̶table_NAMEe1"

INNER JOIN ̶table_NAMEe2" ON ̶table_NAMEe1".column"= ̶table_NAMEe2.column";

Let's say you have the following two tables:

Table A

Students

StudentNo	LastNAMEe	FirstNAMEe	Age	Address	City
1	Potter	Michael	17	130 Reed Ave.	Cheyenne
2	Walker	Jean	18	110 Westlake	Cody
3	Anderson	Ted	18	22 Staten Sq.	Laramie
4	Dixon	Allan	18	12 Glenn Rd.	Casper
5	Cruise	Timothy	19	20 Reed Ave.	Cheyenne

Table B

StudentInformation

StudentNo	Year	Average
1	1st	90
2	1st	87
3	3rd	88
4	5th	77
5	2nd	93

You may want to extract specified data from both tables. Let's say from table A, you want to display LastNAMEe, FirstNAMEe and the City, while from Table B, you want to display the Average.

You can construct your SQL statement this way:

Example:

SELECT Students.LastNAMEe, Students.FirstNAMEe, StudentInformation.AverageFROM Students

INNER JOIN StudentInformation ON Students.StudentNo=StudentInformation.StudentNo;

This SQL query will display these data on your resulting table:

LastNAMEe	FirstNAMEe	Average
Potter	Michael	**90**
Walker	Jean	**87**
Anderson	Ted	**88**
Dixon	Allan	**77**
Cruise	Timothy	**93**

LEFT **OUTER JOIN (LEFT JOIN)** – This SQL statement will display all rows from the left hand table (table 1), even if these do not match with the right hand table (table 2).

With the ON key word, it will display only the rows specified. Data from the other table will only be displayed, if the data intersect with the first selected table.

Let's use the two base tables above and create LEFT JOIN with the tables to display the LastNAMEe and the Year. You can create your SQL statement this way:

Example: SELECT students.LastNAMEe, StudentInformation.Year

FROM students

LEFT JOIN StudentInformation

ON Students.StudentNo

StudentInformation.StudentNo;

Your resulting table will appear this way:

LastNAMEe	Year
Potter	1st
Walker	1st

Anderson	3rd
Dixon	5th
Cruise	2nd

RIGHT OUTER JOIN (RIGHT JOIN) – This query will display all the rows from the right hand table (table2). With the ON key word added, just like with the LEFT JOIN, it will display only the rows specified.

This SQL statement will display all data from table 2, even if there are no matches from table 1 (left table). Take note that only the data from table 1 that intersect with table 2 will be displayed.

Example:

SELECT "column1", "column2" from "table_NAME1" RIGHT (OUTER) JOIN "table_NAME2"

ON "table_NAME1".column" = "table_NAME2.column"

Let's use the same base tables above, to facilitate viewing, the two base tables are shown again on this page

Table A Student

Student No	LastNAMEe	FirstNAMEe	Age	Address	City
1	Potter	Michael	17	130 ReedAve.	Cheyenne
2	Walker	Jean	18	110 Westlake	Cody
3	Anderson	Ted	18	22 StatenSq.	Laramie
4	Dixon	Allan	18	12 Glenn Rd.	Casper
5	Cruise	Timothy	19	20 Reed Ave.	Cheyenne

Table B

StudentInformation

StudentNo	Year	Average

1	1st	90
2	1st	87
3	3rd	88
4	5th	77

And you want to perform a RIGHT OUTER JOIN or a RIGHT JOIN.

Here's how you can state your SQL query.

Example: SELECT Students.City, StudentInformation.Average

FROM Students

RIGHT JOIN StudentInformation

ON students.StudentNo = StudentInformation.StudentNoORDER

BY Students.City;

Your result-table will appear like this:

City	Average
Cheyenne	90

Casper	77
Cheyenne	93
Cody	87
Laramie	88

FULL OUTER JOIN (FULL JOIN) – This SQL keyword will display allthe rows from both the left and right hand tables.

All data should be displayed by a query using these keywords. Take note that you should insert nulls when the conditions are not met in the joined table

Example: SELECT―column1",―column2"from―table_NAMEe1"

FULL (OUTER) JOIN―table_NAMEe2"

ON―table_NAMEe1"."column"="table_NAMEe2"."column";

Using the two base tables above, you can create your SQL FULL JOIN statementthis way:

Example: SELECT Students.LastNAMEe,

StudentInformation.AverageFROM Students

FULL JOIN StudentInformation

ON students.StudentNo = StudentInformation.StudentNoORDER

BY Students.LastNAMEe;

This will be your table output:

LastNAMEe	Average
Potter	90
Anderson	93
Cruise	88
Dixon	87
Walker	77

There are no NULL VALUES in any of the columns because the column in bothtables matched.

- **CROSS JOIN** – This SQL key word will display each row from table1that combined with each row from table2.

This is also called the CARTESIAN JOIN.

xample: SELECT * from [―able_NAMEe1"] CROSS JOIN ―able_NAMEe2"];

sing the two base tables above, we can create a SQL statement this way: Example: ELECT * from Students CROSS JOIN StudentInformation;

Iaking use of this JOIN SQL syntax properly can save time and money. se them to your advantage. Take note that when the WHERE clause is sed, the CROSS JOIN becomes an INNER JOIN.

here is also one way of expressing your CROSS JOIN. The SQL can be eated this way: Example: SELECT LastNAMEe, FirstNAMEe, Age, ddress, City

ROM Students

ROSS JOIN StudentInformation;

here will be slight variations in the SQL statements of other SQL rvers, but the main syntax is typically basic.

HAPTERS 6: SQL JOINS AND UNION

far, we've largely been dealing with clauses that separate data points. NIQUE, DISTINCT, and even restrictions are used to separate data points om one another.

INS and UNIONS are diametrically opposed. Rather than segregating data to different sets, these unite it under one banner.

you recall, we briefly discussed JOINs at the beginning of the book; today, e'll look at them from a less theoretical, more practical perspective.

JOINS

JOINs are SQL's means of combining several data points from N tables and storing them in a database. A JOIN is a method of combining fields from at least two tables by exploiting the values that they share.

An excellent example of how JOIN's function works is:

- ONE TABLE

```
+——+——————————+———-+——————————-+——————————+
SALARY | ID | NAME | AG | ADDRESS |
+——+——————————+———-+——————————-+——————————+
| 1 | Ilija | 19 | Uruguay | 15000.00
2 | Frank | 52 | Tom St | 200.00
| 3 | Jim | 53 | Serbia | 8040.00
| 4 | Martinia | 54 | Amsterdam | 9410.00
Podgorica | 55200.00 | 5 | Jaffar | 66 |
Prune | 1200.00 | 6 | Tim | 33 | Prune | 1200.00 |
```

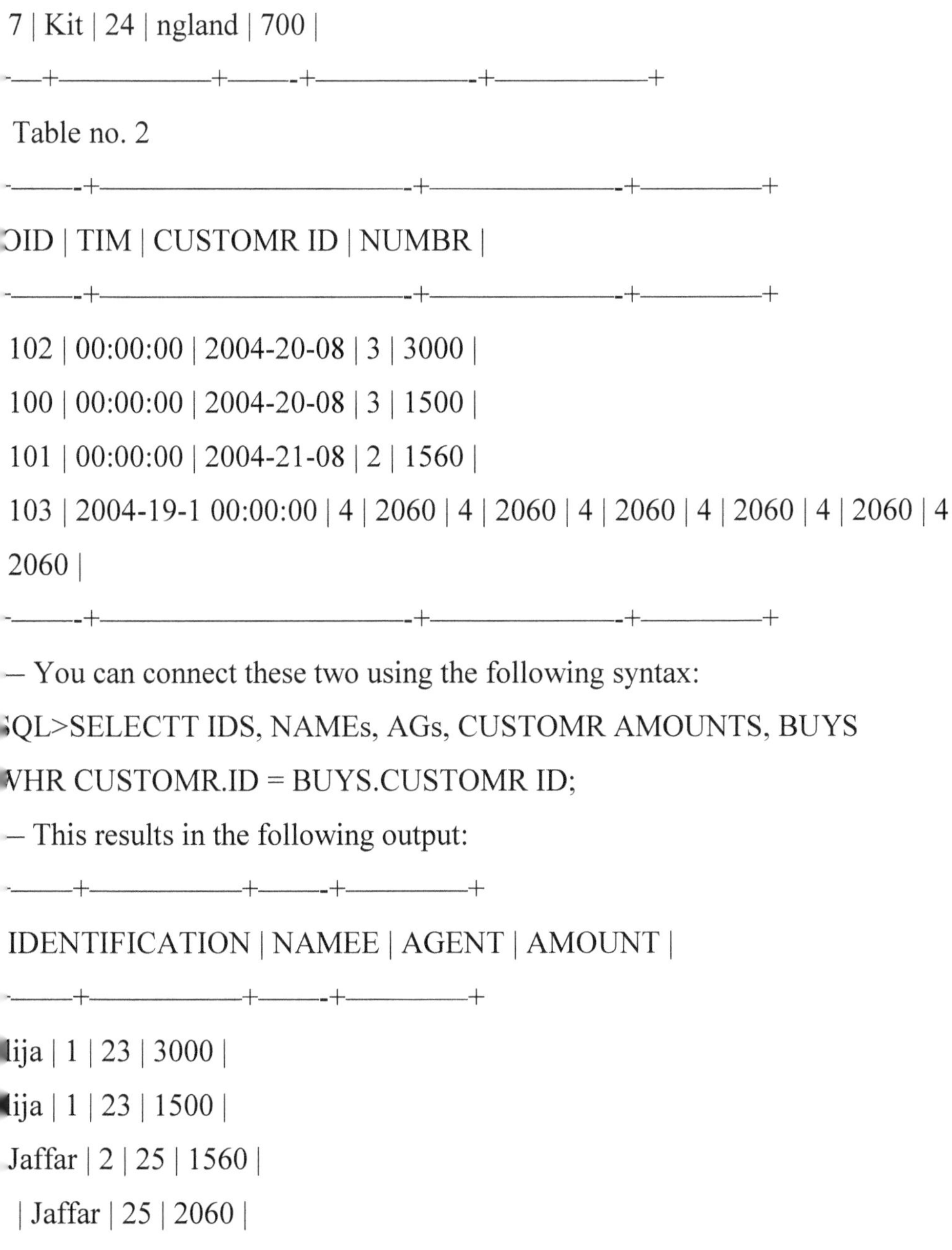

7 | Kit | 24 | ngland | 700 |

-—+——————+——-+——————-+—————+

Table no. 2

-———-+————————————+———————-+——————-+————+

ɔID | TIM | CUSTOMR ID | NUMBR |

-———-+————————————+———————-+——————-+————+

102 | 00:00:00 | 2004-20-08 | 3 | 3000 |

100 | 00:00:00 | 2004-20-08 | 3 | 1500 |

101 | 00:00:00 | 2004-21-08 | 2 | 1560 |

103 | 2004-19-1 00:00:00 | 4 | 2060 | 4 | 2060 | 4 | 2060 | 4 | 2060 | 4 | 2060 | 4

2060 |

-———-+————————————+———————-+——————-+————+

– You can connect these two using the following syntax:

ɔQL>SELECTT IDS, NAMEs, AGs, CUSTOMR AMOUNTS, BUYS

ʌHR CUSTOMR.ID = BUYS.CUSTOMR ID;

– This results in the following output:

-———+——————+———-+————+

IDENTIFICATION | NAMEE | AGENT | AMOUNT |

-———+——————+———-+————+

lija | 1 | 23 | 3000 |

lija | 1 | 23 | 1500 |

Jaffar | 2 | 25 | 1560 |

 | Jaffar | 25 | 2060 |

-———+——————+———-+————+

That was quite simple, wasn't it? JOINs in SQL can be performed in a variety of ways. You can use a variety of operators, ranging from = to! = as well as the greater and lesser symbols You can also use SQL keywords such as BETWEEN and NOT to accomplish this. With that said, the most common operator you'll use is the = sign.

Let's have a look at the variety of JOINs in SQL now, shall we?

Let's begin with the most common join, the INNER JOIN, which is used in practically every larger SQL database and is often referred to as a SQUIJOIN since it treats both of the tables that are being joined equally.

This JOIN creates a new table by simply mixing the values contained in the rows and columns of the tables you're connecting. The JOIN will compare and contrast each row of table 1 to each row of table 2. It will find all rows that can be JOIN-ed, and once that is complete, it will do the same with the columns. The result of a JOIN is simply the sum of these values.

An INNR JOIN has the following syntax:

table01.column01, table02.column02... FROM TABLE 01.

INNR JOIN TABLE 02

ON table01.common field = table02.common field

If you're curious about how this works and what it produces, give it a shot Make two tables and see what the script produces.

Let's have a look at the second join you'll be learning about- the LFT JOIN The LFT JOIN is exactly what it sounds like...left. It serves to output every row from the left table. This means that if the table on the left has members even if there are no ON clause matches in the right one, this JOIN will still provide results. This means that you can combine the left table with an empty table and still get a valid output.

Due to the lack of a fail-safe, this is one of the more difficult connections to debug. The LFT JOIN is defined in the SQL standard as follows:

SELECT   table01.column01,table02.column02...table0N.column0N   FROM table01.

JOIN LFT table02

ON table01.common field = table02.common field

You would put in the ON condition that needs to be fulfilled here, based on what you need to do.

The RIGHT JOIN in SQL is the inverse of the LFT JOIN in that it returns all data from the right table regardless of the number of matches in the left one. This makes it equally as difficult to debug as the LFT JOIN, because you will still get an output even if the ON clause contains no matches. This will just return a NULL value for every column in the table on the left.

This means that the return of the RIGHT JOIN consists of the values from the right side, as well as the matches from the left table.

Its syntax is as follows:

SELECT   table01.column01,table02.column02...table0N.column0N   FROM table01.

JOIN table02 ON THE RIGHT

ON table01.common field = table02.common field

The FULL JOIN in SQL is simply a combination of these two. It will show you all of the records from both the left and right tables. It is the most difficult

JOIN to debug because none of the tables must be filled. You may literally JOIN two tables with no elements in either of them, and the only indication that something is amiss is that it returns entire NULL vales. The syntax for this type of JOIN is as follows:

SELECT   table01.column01,table02.column02...table0N.column0N   FROM table01.

COMPLETE JOIN table02

ON table01.common field = table02.common field

Some databases, such as MySQL, do not support the FULL JOIN; if you find yourself working with one of these heretic machines, you can use the UNION ALL clause to get around this limitation.

Bind the LFT JOIN and RIGHT JOIN together to get the equivalent of a FULL JOIN. The syntax for this is:

SQL> SECTION A, B FROM A

JOIN LFT JOIN B

ALL ON A.ID = B.A ID UNION

SELECT A, B, C, AND D FROM A

JOIN B TO THE RIGHT

B.A ID ON A.ID = B.A ID

The SQL SLF JOIN is intended to connect a given tab to itself, as if it were two tabs. This serves the purpose of modifying the NAMEe of at least one, but up to N, tables in a single SQL statement.

The basic syntax for an SLF Link to join table a to itself is as follows:

ELECTT a.column NAMEe, b.column NAMEe... FROM TABLE01 A AND
TABLE01 B

WHR a.common field = b.common field

- In this case, the WHR clause can be assigned to any type of SQL
execution. It is any condition you wish to join based on, think of it as a
temporary restriction on the vales.

SQL> SLT a.A, b.B, a.A FROM a, b

WHR a.B b.B; WHR a.B b.B;

Next, let's look at the CARTSIAN or CROSS JOIN, which is a type of JOIN
that returns the cross product of two sets of data points. These must be
obtained from at least two, but no more than N tables. This equates it to an
INNR type of JOIN, where the criterion for being joined is always true, or
where there is no JOIN condition in the first place. It has a very simple
syntax:

FROM table01,table02,table03...table0N TO

table01.column01,table02.column02...column0N

That's it! The CARTSIAN JOIN sounds a lot more complicated than it is.

UNIONS

Unions in SQL are clauses that combine the results of at least two, but potentially up to N different SQL statements, while ignoring any possible duplicate entries.

Now, you can't use a UNION clause for every SELECTT statement out there, there are a few conditions they must first meet:

- The duality of SELECTTs must have the same number of selected columns.

- Each column in the SELECTT statements must have the exact same numerical value corresponding to the expression count inside it.

- All columns in the SELECTT statements must have the same data type.

- Every column in the SELECTT statistics must have its data points in the same order. It should be noted that they do not have to be the same length.

This means that you can UNION a 0.02 float and a 20 float. There is a general syntax for the UNION operation, which is as follows:

SELECT column01 [, column02] FROM table01 [, table02] [WHR your_condition] SELECT column01 [, table02]

—your condition refers to the condition you've set up for the UNION-ing of these two select statements.

UNION

SELECT column01 [, column02] FROM table01 [, table02] [WHR your condition] SELECT column01 [, table02]

—Now, consider how one of these would look in practise, substituting columns and tables for A,B, and so on.

SQL> SECT A, B, C, AND D FROM TABLA

LFT JOIN TABLB WHERE A.ID = B.B ID

UNION

LFT JOIN TABLB ON A.ID = B.B ID SELECTTA A, B, C, D FROM TABLA LFT JOIN TABLB ON A.ID = B.B ID

That's the gist of it! Hopefully, it will help you remember the UNION statements better. Next, let's have a look at the UNION ALL clause. This operator serves to combine the outcomes of two SELECTT statements, similar to the previous clause, except that this one also includes duplicate rows.

The rules that govern the UNION ALL clause are the same as those that govern the UNION clause:

The duality of SELECTTs must have the same number of selected columns.

- Each column in the SELECTT statements must have the exact same numerical value corresponding to the expression count inside it.

- All columns in the SELECTT statements must have the same data type.

- Every column in the SELECTT statistics must have its data points in the same order. It should be noted that they do not have to be the same length. This means that you can UNION ALL of a 0.02 float with a 20 float.

The fundamental syntax behind UNION ALL is as follows, with an example

SELECTT column01 [, column02]

[WHR your condition] FROM table01 [, table02]

ALL UNION

SELECT column01 [, column02] FROM table01 [, table02] [WHR your condition] SELECT column01 [, table02]

SQL> SECT A, B, C, AND D FROM A

JOIN LFT JOIN B

SELECTT A, B, C, D ON A.ID = B.A ID

FROM A, JOIN B TO THE RIGHT

B.A ID ON A.ID = B.A ID

The INTRSCT and XCPT operators are two more operators that behave similarly to UNION clauses in SQL.

The simplest approach to think about these would be from the position of set theory. In set theory, the two UNION's are unions of sets, whilst the INTRSCT and XCPT act exactly as they would in set theory. The INTRSCT operator will return the elements that are the same in both the first and second

SELECTT statements. Consider it as demonstrating what two tables have in common.

The general syntax for an INTRSCT statement is as follows:

SELECT column01 [, column02] FROM table01 [, table02] [WHR your_ condition] SELECT column01 [, table02]

—your condition refers to the condition you've set up for the UNION-ing of these two select statements.

INTERSECT

SELECT column01 [, column02] FROM table01 [, table02] [WHR your condition] SELECT column01 [, table02]

—Now, consider how one of these would look in practise, substituting the columns and rows.

Tables for A,B, and so on.

SQL> SECT A, B, C, AND D FROM TABLA

LFT JOIN TABLB WHERE A.ID = B.B ID

INTERSECT

LFT JOIN TABLB ON A.ID = B.B ID SELECTTA A, B, C, D FROM TABLA LFT JOIN TABLB ON A.ID = B.B ID

The XCPT operator is the inverse of the INTRSCT one. While the INTRSCT operator outputs what two SELECTT statements share, the XCPT operator outputs their

differences. It is governed by the same rules as the UNION operator and is not supported by MySQL. The syntax is as follows:

SELECT column01 [, column02] FROM table01 [, table02] [WHR your_ condition] SELECT column01 [, table02]

—your condition refers to the condition you've set up for the UNION-ing of these two select statements.

EXCEPT

SELECT column01 [, column02] FROM table01 [, table02] [WHR your condition] SELECT column01 [, table02]

—Now, consider how one of these would look in practise, substituting the columns and rows.

Tables for A,B, and so on.

SQL> SECT A, B, C, AND D FROM TABLA

LFT JOIN TABLB WHERE A.ID = B.B ID

EXCEPT

LFT JOIN TABLB ON A.ID = B.B ID SELECTTA A, B, C, D FROM TABLA LFT JOIN TABLB ON A.ID = B.B ID

Finally, we'll take a look at a special case. The SQL NULL value is used to represent a value that has not yet been declared. Any NULL values within a table will be displayed as blank. If a field has the value null, it means it has no value, but not in the same way that 0 does. For example, the number of extra heads you have is 0, but the number of unicorns you have might be 0, but it could also be more, making it null.

It's critical to remember that the NULL operator is quite problematic. It's frowned upon to use NULL in places where it isn't expressly required. This is due to the fact that it can result in certain rather buggy scenarios.

/hen it comes to actually using the NULL operator, the value will always be
nknown, and will generally be excluded from whatever results you acquire.
o determine whether a value is NULL, you must use the IS NULL or IS
OT NULL operators.

or the final SQL topic in this chapter, we'll look at aliases. An alias in SQL
 analogous to an alias in real life. In the same manner that James Bond has
07, your TABL 1 might have my table NAMEe (as you can tell, I'm not very
eative when it comes to variable NAMEes). This reNAMEing is only
mporary and will not change the NAMEe of the table in the database. In
eneral, aliases are used to save space and make time coding easier. The
eneral syntax for an alias is as follows:

ELECT column 01, column 02...

/HR [your condition] FROM NAMEe of table AS alias of table NAMEe;

- The SQL snippet below demonstrates how to use aliases in practise.

QL> SELECTTA.ID, A.NAMES, A.AGS, B.AMOUNTS FROM A AS C,
RDERRS AS B

.A ID = WHR C.ID;

–Here's how to use a column alias:

QL> FROM A, SECT ID AS A, NAME AS B

/HR C DOES NOT EXIST;

NION and ALL UNION

 SQL, you may use the union operator to combine the results of two or more
ieries. These are very select statements. Before we go into the syntax, there
e a few things you should keep in mind:

- The SELECT statements in a UNION should always have the same number of columns.

- Every column should have the same data type.

- Every statement's columns should be in the same order.

CHAPTER 7. TRANSACTIONS IN SQL SERVER

This chapter will teach you how to use three common SQL transaction commands with SQLiteStudio: COMMIT, ROLLBACK, and SAVPOINT. Controlling such transactions necessitates that the user manage certain database changes that are typically caused by DML commands (insert, update, and delete).

When a database transaction is successfully executed, the data or structure of the table will definitely be altered. During the execution of a transaction, information is stored in a temporary database space, also known as a rollback area. Execute the appropriate transaction command to finalise these transactions and permanently save the changes made to the database. The rollback area is only emptied after this process.

COMMIT

The SQL COMMIT statement is in charge of storing all transactions to a database. This command was also encountered in Chapter 6 via the COMMIT CHANGES STRUCTUR button (when a copy of the Customer TBL table was created). You will now use SQLiteStudio to manipulate the Customer

TBL table structure by adding a new record in the GRID VIW mode

By picking the option, you may get to the SQL EDITOR. To enter the following programming line in the QUERY tab and click the EEXCUTE QUERY button to end all the transactions currently operating in the database:

Click the cell containing **CustomerID = 5**, which is the last row of the firs column in the table.

Choose the **PLACE NEW ROWS BELOW SELECTED ROW** option from the dropdown arrow that is beside the **INSERT ROW (INS)** button.To see the new empty row added to the table, click the **INSERT ROW (INS)** butt

Add the data values below in the new table record:

CustomerID: 6

	Structure	Data	Constraints	Indexes	Triggers	DDL

	CustomerID	CustomerName	JobPosition	CompanyName	USStat
1	1	KATHY ALE	President	Tile Industrial	TX
2	2	KEVIN LORD	Vice-President	Best Tooling	NY
3	3	KIM ASH	Director	Car World	CA
4	4	ABBY KARR	Manager	West Mart	NV
5	5	MIKE ARMHS	Vice-President	1 Driving School	NJ

To permanently store the new data values added, click the COMMIT button

ROLLBACK

The SQL ROLLBACK statement is the reverse of the COMMIT command, in which all unsaved changes are discarded. Transactions, on the other hand, can only be undone since the previous COMMIT or ROLLBACK statement that was executed.

Syntax:

[WORK] ROLLBACK;

Furthermore, before executing a ROLLBACK command, ensure that the transactions have already begun.

Syntax:

TRANSACTION ON BEGIN;

To demonstrate how a ROLLBACK statement works in SQLiteStudio, modify the DROP TABL command:

Go to the QUERY tab after selecting the choice. nter the following programming line, then click the EEXCUTEE QUERY button:

TRANSACTION ON BEGIN;

Return to the SQL DITOR and clear out the QUERY tab. This time, type the following code and then click the EXCUTE QUERY button. The Customer TBL table will be removed from the TABLS list as a result of this.

Customer TABLE; DROP TABLE;

Erase the content of the QUERY tab once more and type the following command statement. Please visit the QUERY button with EEXCUTEE. This will reverse the deletion of the Customer TBL table.

ROLLBACK;

To see if the ROLLBACK command was successfully executed, right-click anywhere inside the window.

DATABASE NAVIGATOR pane, then choose REFRESH ALL DATABAS SCHMAS.

Now, in the left pane, select the TABL list to see if the Customer TBL table has returned.

Command SAVEPOINT

The SQL SAVPOINT statement is used when you want to reverse a specific transaction back to a specific point rather than the entire database transaction. This is done before a ROLLBACK action. You will be able to manage several transactions by breaking them down into smaller pieces of SQL statements in this manner.

Syntax:

SAVPOINT NAME

You can also combine the SAVPOINT and ROLLBACK commands. Syntax:

RETURN TO SAVPOINT NAME;

The NAMEe of the database object (on which the SQL transactions will be performed) can be used as a savepoint NAMEe. However, they should be distinct from the set of transactions that you intend to divide into segments (or points). To demonstrate how a SAVPOINT with a ROLLBACK command works, first delete certain records from the Customer TBL table and reverse this database transaction.

lick the choice and enter the code below in the QUERY tab. click the
XCUTE QUERY

utton:

RANSACTION ON BEGIN;

elete the QUERY tab's contents, type the following code, and click the
XCUTE QUERY button. This will create a savepoint section before
moving the final record from the Customer TBL table.

ustomer SP1 SAVPOINT;

lear out the QUERY tab once more to remove the last record from the
ustomer TBL table. Then enter the following programming line and press
e EXCUTE QUERY button:

ELETE FROM Customerer TBL WHR CustomerID = 6;

o see if the record has been removed, double-click the Customer TBL tab
ider the TABLS list in the DATABAS NAVIGATOR pane on the left. Go
 the GRID VIW tab by clicking the DATA tab on the right. Then, on the
eyboard, press F5 to access the REFRESH TABL DATA button. You should
e a table that looks like this:

ow, select the option again to clear the QUERY tab. Then enter the
llowing programming line and press the EXCUTE QUERY button to create
e second savepoint section (this is done before deleting the record where the
ustomerID=5).

ustomer SP2 SAVPOINT;

Clear off the QUERY tab and type the following line of code to delete th customer record with the CustomerID=5. Then click the EXCUTE QUER button:

DELETE FROM Customer TBL WHR CustomererID=5;

Check to see if the customer record was deleted by clicking the option at th bottom left corner of the screen. Click the DATA tab on the right, and the under the GRID VIW tab, click the REFRESH TABL DATA button (or F5 o the keyboard). The table you'll see should be the same as the one below:

Now, reversing the last transaction, select the option again and eras everything inside the QUEQUERY tab. After you've typed the followin programming line, click the EXCUTE QUERY button:

RETURN TO Customer SP2;

To see if the deleted record has been reversed, click option, then the DAT. tab on the right. Click the GRID VIW tab and then the REFRESH TAB DATA button (press F5 on the keyboard). Your table should have the sam data values as the one below:

Clear the QUERY tab, enter the following programming line, and then clic the EXCUTE QUERY button to reverse a transaction where a record was fir deleted:

RETURN TO Customer SP1;

To verify if the record deletion was reversed, click the option and then th DATA tab in the right pane. Go to the GRID VIW tab, then click th REFRESH TABL DATA button (or F5 on the keyboard). Before any of th deletion transactions, the table should look exactly like the original one.